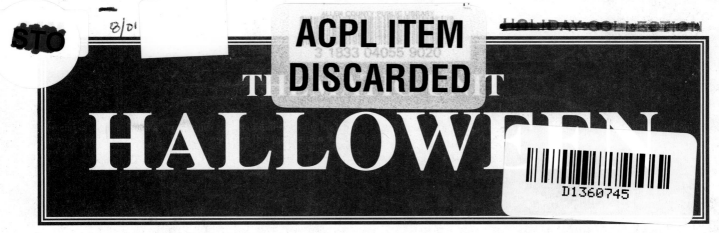

THE BEST OF

HALLOWEEN

Written by Ireta Sitts Graube and Jeanne King

Illustrated by Sue Fullam, Keith Vasconcelles, and Theresa Wright

Teacher Created Materials, Inc.
6421 Industry Way
Westminster, CA 92683
www.teachercreated.com

©1996 Teacher Created Materials, Inc.
Reprinted, 2001
Made in U.S.A.
ISBN-1-55734-257-1

Table of Contents

Introduction 3

History of Halloween 5

Corduroy's Halloween by Don Freeman and B.G. Hennessy (Penguin Books, New York, 1995) . . 7
(Available in Canada, Penguin; U.K and AUS, Penguin Ltd.)
    Summary—Sample Plan—Overview of Activities—Pumpkin Get Acquainted Game—
    Paint a Pumpkin Still Life—Corduroy's Costume Clues—Graphing, Weighing, and
    Measuring—Lift-the Flap Patterns—Halloween Mystery Box

The Biggest Pumpkin Ever by Steven Kroll (Holiday House, 1984) 18
(Available in Canada, U.K., and Australia from Scholastic, Inc.)
    Summary—Sample Plan—Overview of Activities—Sharing Is Fun—Listening Skills—
    Mouse Math Measurement—Food Collage—Pumpkin Seed Growth Experiment—Paper
    Bag Puppet—Paper Mouse Characters

Arthur's Halloween by Marc Brown (Little, Brown & Co., 1982) 29
(Available in Canada, U.K, and Australia from Little, Brown & Co.)
    Summary—Sample Plan—Overview of Activities—Small History Book—Halloween
    Wordo—Dot-to-Dot Math—Create a Haunted House

Poetry & Writing Activities 37
    Frame It!—Pumpkin Poetry Frame—Making New Rhymes from Old—Overview of
    Journal Writing—Journal Writing Ideas—Halloween Writing Projects

Across the Curriculum 43
    Language Arts: Alphabetical Halloween—Halloween Adjectives—Halloween Syllables—
                               Clayton and I Are Friends—How to Make Big Books—How to Make
                               Little Books—Pop Up Books
    Math: Halloween Math Facts Game—Trick-or-Treat Math—Bat Math
    Science: Fall Leaves Me Colder—Fall Leaves Me Colorful—Halloween
                               Experiments: Scary Ticking Noises, Pumpkin Sounds, Halloween Money
    Social Studies: Trick-or-Treating
    Art: Drawing Halloween Characters—Halloween Weaving—Witch's Mask—
                               Watercolor Witch's Hat—3-D Ghost—Tissue Paper Goblin
    Music: Songs: "Corduroy's Fall Song," "Sharing in Our Class," "Sharing with
                               My Neighbor," "Witches, Black Cats, Scary Goblins," "Zip-A-Dee-Do-
                               Dah Halloween."
    Life Skills: Halloween Mouse Cookies—Goblin Doughouts—Pumpkin Milkshakes—
                               Pumpkin Cake—Cooking a Pumpkin—Steamed and Baked Pumpkin
                               Seeds

Culminating Activities 72
    Halloween Vegetable Carving—Cooperative Halloween Mini-Plays

Unit Management 74
    Letters to Parents—Awards—Halloween Learning Centers—Halloween Clip Art—Halloween
    Stationery

Bibliography 80

Introduction

Halloween contains a captivating whole language, thematic unit. Its 80 exciting pages are filled with a wide variety of lesson ideas and activities designed for use with primary children. At its core are three high-quality children's literature selections, *The Biggest Pumpkin Ever, Corduroy's Halloween,* and *Arthur's Halloween.* For each of these books, activities are included which set the stage for reading, encourage the enjoyment of the book, and extend the concepts gained. In addition, the theme is connected to the curriculum with activities in language arts (including daily writing suggestions), math, science, social studies, art, music, and life skills. Many of these activities encourage cooperative learning. Furthermore, directions for student-created Big Books and culminating activities, which allow students to synthesize their knowledge in order to produce products that can be shared beyond the classroom, highlight this very complete teacher resource.

This thematic unit includes:

❑ **literature selections**—summaries of three children's books with related lessons (complete with reproducible pages) that cross the curriculum.

❑ **poetry**—suggested selections and lessons enabling students to write and publish their own works

❑ **planning guides**—suggestions for sequencing lessons each day of the unit

❑ **writing and language experience ideas**—daily suggestions as well as writing activities across the curriculum, including Big Books

❑ **bulletin board ideas**—suggestions throughout the unit for student-created and/or interactive bulletin boards

❑ **homework suggestions**—extending the unit to the child's home

❑ **curriculum connections**—in language arts, math, science, social studies, art, music, and life skills

❑ **group projects**—to foster cooperative learning

❑ **a culminating activity**—which requires students to synthesize their learning to produce a product or engage in an activity that can be shared with others

❑ **a bibliography**—suggesting additional literature and nonfiction books on the theme.

> **To keep this valuable resource intact so that it can be used year after year, you may wish to punch holes in the pages and store them in a three-ring binder.**

Introduction *(cont.)*

Why Whole Language?

A whole language approach involves children in using all modes of communication: reading, writing, listening, observing, illustrating, experiencing, and doing. Communication skills are interconnected and integrated into lessons that emphasize the whole of language rather than isolating its parts. The lessons revolve around selected literature. Reading is not taught as a separate subject from writing and spelling, for example. A child reads, writes (spelling appropriately for his/her level), speaks, listens, etc. in response to a literature experience introduced by the teacher. In this way, language skills grow naturally, stimulated by involvement and interest in the topic at hand.

Why Thematic Planning?

One very useful tool for implementing an integrated whole language program is thematic planning. By choosing a theme with correlating literature selections for a unit of study, a teacher can plan activities throughout the day that lead to a cohesive, in-depth study of the topic. Students will be practicing and applying their skills in meaningful contexts. Consequently, they tend to learn and retain more. Both teachers and students will be freed from a day that is broken into unrelated segments of isolated drill and practice.

Why Cooperative Learning?

Besides academic skills and content, students need to learn social skills. No longer can this area of development be taken for granted. Students must learn to work cooperatively in groups in order to function well in modern society. Group activities should be a regular part of school life and teachers should consciously include social objectives as well as academic objectives in their planning. For example, a group working together to write a report may need to select a leader. The teacher should make clear to the students and monitor the qualities of good leader-follower group interaction just as he/she would state and monitor the academic goals of the projects.

Why Big Books?

Big Books serve as excellent cooperative learning projects for children. They allow children to gain experience in reading, writing, spelling, and illustrating. Because of their size, Big Books are easily shared with groups of children or the entire class. There are several suggestions for Big Books throughout this thematic unit.

Why Journals?

Each day your students should have the opportunity to write in a journal. They may respond to a book, write about a personal experience or answer a general "question of the day" posed by the teacher. Students should be encouraged to refer to the posted vocabulary list to check their spelling. Teachers may read journals every day or choose to alternate days for boys and girls. This cumulative journal provides an excellent means of documenting writing progress.

History of Halloween

(The following information on the history of Halloween is provided as a teacher resource.)
Halloween is celebrated on October 31st. Its origin goes far back in history to the time of the Celtic people. They lived more than two thousand years ago in parts of France and the British Isles.

The Celtic people had many gods. One of those gods was Samhain, (pronounced Sa-wen) Lord of the Dead. They believed he came back to earth on October 31st, which was their New Year's Eve. When he came back he brought all the dead with him. Priests, called Druids, made large bonfires and burned animals for Samhain. They believed the sacrifices would please him and inspire him to give them good luck. The Celts also put out food and gifts on their doorsteps in hopes that it would please Samhain. They also hoped the bonfires would frighten away the ghosts of the dead. Some of the Celts wore costumes made from animals' heads and furs. They felt it would be wise to disguise themselves so the spirits would not recognize them.

Roman armies invaded the British Isles and France in the year 43, and made them part of the Roman Empire. The Romans had different gods but they also had a festival for the dead in late October. Another festival in early November honored Pomona, the goddess of orchards and fruit. This was a happy festival. Pomona especially liked apples, so apples were given to the gods in thanks for the farmers' crops. The Romans ruled the Celts for about 400 years and during that time the three holidays became blended into one.

In the fourth century, the Romans declared Christianity lawful. Christian fathers tried to stamp out all the old religions and their holidays. The Celts, who were now celebrating a mixture of the three holidays, were difficult to convince, so the church set aside All Saint's Day in memory of all the early Christians who died for their beliefs. This was later celebrated on November 1st. Another name for All Saint's Day was All Hallows. October 31st was known as All Hallow's Even, which means "holy evening." This was later abbreviated to Halloween. Halloween, All Saint's Day, and the Celtic celebration of Samhain were all celebrated around the same time and had much in common. Some people merged them all together.

When the Scottish and the Irish came to the United States in the nineteenth century they brought Halloween with them. This Halloween was a mixture of many centuries of religious beliefs.

Witches were an important part of the Halloween celebration. The name witch comes from the Saxon word wica and means the wise one. In Scotland, people believed that all witches met on Halloween and danced all night. The witches dressed up like animals and their dances were to encourage fertility in human beings and animals. In some of the dances they galloped with branches or broomsticks between their legs. As they danced, they chanted.

History of Halloween *(cont.)*

Black cats are also a symbol of Halloween and we find that cats have been treasured and feared in many cultures down through the ages. The Egyptians worshiped a cat-headed goddess named "Pasht." Many pieces of jewelry were carved with cat heads and cats eyes. The Druids believed that cats were humans changed into cats by evil powers. They threw cats on their bonfires during their sacrifices to Samhain.

As time went on, most educated people did not believe in witches, witchcraft, or witches' cats. Those who still believed in their existence sought ways to keep them away. Scottish farmers carried flaming sticks of fire from east to west across their fields. They hoped the sticks would burn the witches' brooms as they flew over. The Pennsylvania Dutch farmers painted hex signs on their barns to scare away the witches.

Iron and salt were put in the bed of a newborn baby to scare away the witches. People believed that witches would not touch iron or salt.

Corduroy's Halloween

by Don Freeman and B.G. Hennessy

Summary

Corduroy, the stuffed bear, has another adventure in this delightful "lift-a-flap" book based on Don Freeman's popular character. In this story, Corduroy prepares for Halloween fun and adventure. The book opens with a celebration of autumn and continues with pumpkin carving, trick-or-treating, creating costumes, and more. The illustrations are vibrant, and the hidden pictures are plentiful. Young learners will delight in this playful book.

The outline below is a suggested plan for using the various activities that are presented in this unit. You should adapt these ideas to fit your own classroom situations.

Sample Plan

Day 1

- Set up Learning Center (page 77).
- Play Pumpkin Get Acquainted Game (page 11).
- Make predictions about the book (page 8).
- Read *Corduroy's Halloween.*
- Start journal writing (pages 40-41).
- Introduce Halloween Mystery Box (page 17).
- Sing "Corduroy's Fall Song" (page 67).

Day 2

- Review *Corduroy's Halloween* and discuss predictions made on Day 1.
- Make list of real and imaginary animals you found in the book.
- Continue journal writing (page 8).
- Share the Halloween Mystery Box (page 17).
- Brainstorm the signs of autumn (page 9).
- Begin Fall Leaves Me Colder activity (pages 54 and 55).

Day 3

- Write and illustrate a class Big Book (page 9).
- Share the Halloween Mystery Box (page 17).
- Write with open-ended sentence strips (page 42).
- Do the math graphing activities (page 14).
- Make Pumpkin Milkshakes (page 70).

Day 4

- Make Little Books (page 10).
- Share the Halloween Mystery Box (page 17).
- Complete Fall Leaves Me Colorful activity (pages 56 and 57).
- Paint a Pumpkin Still Life (page 12).
- Do Corduroy's Costume Clues (page 13).
- Practice "Corduroy's Fall Song" and make up additional verses.

Day 5

- Illustrate Little Books.
- Play A Sack Full of Sounds game (page 9).
- Continue Fall Leaves Me Colder activity (page 55).
- Share the Halloween Mystery Box (page 17).
- Do Halloween Weaving (page 64).
- Act out the story, using creative dramatics and singing the song.

Overview of Activities

Setting the Stage

1. Prepare your classroom for this unit on Halloween. Set up Learning Centers (page 77). Send home a letter to parents, explaining the unit and requesting materials (page 75).

2. Decorate a box with Halloween decorations from page 78. Use the box with the Halloween Mystery Box activity on page 17. Assign each student a time to take home the Halloween Mystery Box. Have the student fill it with a Halloween item. Ask each student to complete the activity page and use it to guide classmates in guessing what item is in the box. Provide a schedule for sharing the Halloween items with the class.

3. Make numbered paper pumpkins for the Get Acquainted Game on page 11. Use this activity to encourage social interaction and to help create a climate for group projects.

4. Show the class the cover of *Corduroy's Halloween* and make predictions about the story. Ask the following questions: What do you think this book will be about? What will happen to Corduroy in this story? Who else do you think we will meet? Write these predictions on chart paper and refer to them later.

Enjoying the Book

1. Read *Corduroy's Halloween* to the class. Ask students to name the events in the story. Place responses on sentence strips and have students sequence them in a pocket chart or on a flannel board or magnetic board.

2. Refer to the class predictions chart. Relate predictions to what really happened in the story.

3. Brainstorm and chart the signs that remind us that autumn is here and winter is coming (e.g. colder, wetter, weather changes, leaves turning color, pumpkins ripening, etc.). Play some environmental music that will spur students' imaginations. Encourage students to think of all the sounds, smells, tastes, sights, and feelings of autumn.

4. Introduce Journal Writing using the information on page 40. Have students create and personalize their own journals. The journals may be used throughout the unit. Encourage students to write in their journals about how they can tell autumn is here. As an additional journal writing activity, ask students to write another story about Corduroy's trick-or-treating adventures.

5. Use the graphing activities on page 14 to create a number of pictographs that can be displayed throughout the room. Use the sample discussion questions to familiarize students with math language (e.g., all together, how many more/fewer, the difference between).

6. Make and enjoy Pumpkin Milkshakes using the recipe on page 70. Ask students to make predictions about the shade or color they think the milkshakes will be.

7. Ask students to review what signs tell Corduroy that fall has arrived. Point out that two of the first things Corduroy notices are that the air is getting colder and the leaves are changing color. Ask students why they think these things happen. Over the next two weeks, complete the Fall Leaves Me Colder activities on pages 54 and 55.

Overview of Activities *(cont.)*

Enjoying the Book *(cont.)*

8. Create a large tree bulletin board for the Fall Leaves Me Colorful activity on pages 56 and 57. Students cut out the brainstorm leaves and staple them in and around the tree.

9. Play A Sack Full of Sounds. Have a variety of small stuffed animals on hand. Hide one in a paper bag and write the letter that the animal's name begins with on the bag. Encourage the students to guess which animal is in the bag. When they guess correctly, show them the animal and ask them to give the animal a first name that begins with the same letter, such as Barney Bear or Rachel Rabbit. As the children suggest names, write their suggestions on the overhead and have them vote for their favorite name, or each child may write a story about the animal.

10 Sing "Corduroy's Fall Song" (page 67). Add movements and new verses.

Extending the Book

1. Make a Big Book of the story. Let the children help you make this abbreviated form of the story. See page 45 for ideas on making Big Books. It might read something like this:

   Page 1   Fall is here, and it's time for Corduroy to get ready for Halloween.
   Page 2   Corduroy visits the pumpkin patch.
   Page 3   Next, Corduroy goes to the store.
   Page 4   Today is the window painting contest.
   Page 5   Halloween is here. Corduroy's friends trick-or-treat for UNICEF.
   Page 6   Gorduroy joins the Halloween parade.
   Page 7   It's time for the Halloween party. There are doughnuts and cider for everyone!
   Page 8   Happy Halloween!

   Have the students illustrate the pages. Bind the book. Read the new book to the class and make it available for overnight check out.

2. Make Little Books using the same or similar text as in the Big Book. See page 46 for directions on how to make a Little Book. Use some of the Halloween patterns in this unit as illustrations or have students draw their own pictures. Lift-the-flap patterns are provided on page 16. Cut along the dotted lines.

3. Send for the UNICEF (United Nations Children's Fund) orange collection cartons so students can collect donations for UNICEF for Halloween. Students will also receive Halloween safety tips on bookmarks. You must enclose a large, self-addressed, stamped envelope.

   Write to: U.S. Committee for UNICEF
   Group Programs
   Department 2044P
   333 East 38th Street
   New York, NY 10016
   1-800-252-5437

Ask for Trick-or-Treat for UNICEF collection cartons and safety-tips bookmarks.

Overview of Activities *(cont.)*

Extending the Book *(cont.)*

4. Paint Pumpkin Still Lifes as shown on page 12. This same technique can be used for painting other things, such as the children's stuffed animals that they bring to class during this study. Completed still lifes may be cut out and used for bulletin boards, or you might have the students make up stories to go with their pictures.

5. Decorate the room with 3-D Ghosts for the Culminating Activities (pages 72 and 73). Directions and materials for making the ghosts are found on page 66.

6. Have students experience how to prepare fresh pumpkin. Page 71 provides directions for this activity.

7. Students can create story sequels, review and sequence story events, and practice sentence completion, using open-ended sentences from the story. Suggestions on how to use sentence strips as a writing activity are provided on page 42.

8. Have students use logic to decide which costume is Corduroy's with Corduroy's Costume Clues on page 13.

9. Use the Halloween Weaving activity on page 64 to create placemats or to use as bulletin board backgrounds for displaying student work.

Pumpkin Get Acquainted Game

Directions: If you are finding that some children still do not know each other's names, play this get acquainted game. Duplicate and cut out the pumpkin boxes below for each student in the class. Mark every two pumpkins with the same number. (Make enough pumpkins so that a pair of students will have the same number written on their pumpkins.) Play some Halloween music or marching music and let the children walk around until the music stops. Have children find another child whose pumpkin has the same number and introduce themselves. Exchange pumpkins so that each student receives a new pumpkin and play again.

Variations: Number the pumpkins from 1–4 and let the children form groups. Ask students if they can name everyone in their group. Or, use the activity to help students find out each other's ages, favorite foods, interests, etc.

Instead of pumpkins, use cats, ghosts, or bats and play a musical record on a slow speed. (The strange sounds will create a Halloween atmosphere.)

Paint a Pumpkin Still Life

Materials:

- pumpkins
- newspapers for covering desks
- 12" x 18" (30 cm x 45 cm) paper
- watercolor paints
- paintbrushes
- water and containers for cleaning brushes
- old shirts or smocks to cover clothing
- lamp
- large table
- leaves
- pretty tablecloth or sheet

Directions:

1. Arrange the pumpkins and leaves in the front of the classroom so that each student has a clear view of them.

2. Place the lamp to the side and behind the pumpkins to provide shading on the pumpkins.

3. Show some examples of still-life paintings. Ask the students to note details from the pictures. What do they notice most?

4. Explain that many great artists paint still-life paintings, and today they will be Halloween artists.

5. Give children the necessary equipment and shirts or smocks to protect their clothing. Have them paint the pumpkins and leaves.

6. Hang the paintings in the classroom. If possible, make cardboard frames for the paintings and name/title plaques like one might find in an art gallery or museum.

Variation: Have students bring in stuffed animals, leaves, and small pumpkins of their own to paint. Experiment with pastels, colored pencils, or other coloring implements.

12

Corduroy's Costume Clues

Corduroy and his friends are going trick-or-treating. Can you guess whose costume is whose? Use the clues below to figure out which costumes Corduroy and his friends will be wearing for Halloween.

	ghost	witch	dragon
Corduroy			
Ashley			
Joshua			

Clues:

1. Ashley's costume has a pointed hat.
2. Joshua's costume is not the ghost.
3. Corduroy has a costume that does not show his hands.

Bonus: On the back of this page, draw your Halloween costume.

Teacher: Cover these answers before duplicating.
Corduroy is a ghost, Joshua is a dragon, and Ashley is a witch.

Graphing, Weighing, and Measuring

Use these graphing activities to encourage students to think in math terms. You may wish to create a variety of large graphs to display in the classroom or laminate a large tagboard graph with four or five columns that can be used throughout the year. Cut out small 3" (7.5 cm) squares for each student. You may have them draw pictures on these graph squares or simply write their names. These also make excellent story ideas.

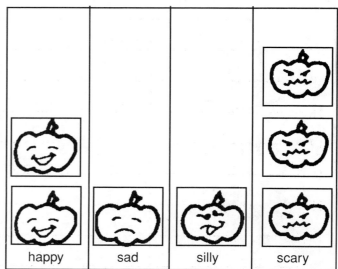

1. Will your jack-o-lantern be happy/sad/silly/scary?

2. Have you ever been to a haunted house? (yes or no)

3. Is your costume friendly/scary/silly?

When you have completed a graph, ask discussion questions such as these.

1. How many fewer students have happy pumpkins than sad ones?

2. How many more students have friendly costumes than silly ones?

3. How many students all together have happy and silly costumes?

You can also have the students do a variety of activities regarding estimation. Here are three.

1. Bring a pumpkin into the classroom. Ask the students to estimate how many seeds they will find in the pumpkin. Write their responses on the board. Create a graph of their responses, like the one shown below. Ask a parent to come in and carve and separate the seeds from the pulp. Count the seeds into small cups in groups of ten.

III	THL I	IIII	THL II	THL THL
0-25	26-50	51-75	76-100	101-125

2. Ask the students to guess how much a pumpkin weighs before carving. Write down and graph their responses. Weigh the pumpkin. Were they over or under?

3. Pass around a ball of string. Have the students cut a piece of string that they believe will fit a pumpkin at its thickest part. Have the students measure the string with rulers and write their estimates and names on their 3" (7.5 cm) cards. Graph their estimates.

Graphing, Weighing, and Measuring *(cont.)*

The graph below may be used as an extension for any of the graphing activities on the previous page. Write in a question at the top and fill in the graphing categories. The students can then color in one square per response. This work sheet can also be used for other themes throughout the year.

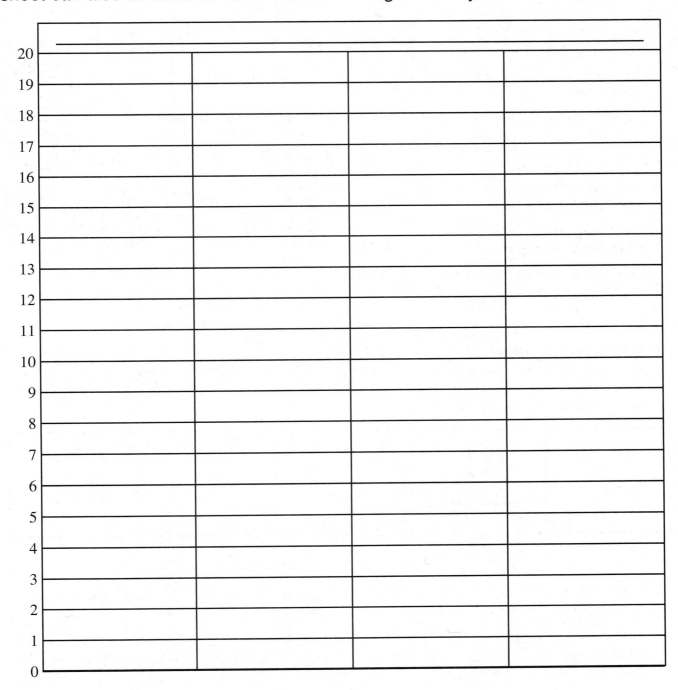

Lift-the-Flap Patterns

These patterns may be used for decorating the room, making Big or Little Books, or as a part of the students' illustrations for their writing or other related projects. Glue each covering picture at the tab only.

Name _____

Halloween Mystery Box

Use the following activity sheet to help you share your Halloween Mystery Box with the class. Place a Halloween item in the class Mystery Box. Write down three clues about your Halloween item. Read one clue at a time and let three children make guesses about the item. If no one guesses, read the next clue. Continue until all clues have been read.

My Clues

1. _____

2. _____

3. _____

Draw a picture of your item in the frame above.
The Mystery Box and this activity sheet must be returned on _____ .

Teacher Note: As an extension, use this activity all year and vary the themes. Or, use no theme and let children bring in any item that will fit in the box. Ask the children to use complete sentences when asking or answering questions about the items in the box.

The Biggest Pumpkin Ever
by Steven Kroll
Summary

A village mouse and a field mouse are both watering and feeding the same pumpkin, unaware of each other. They each have different plans for the pumpkin. The village mouse wants to enter it in the town pumpkin contest. The field mouse wants to make it into the biggest jack-o-lantern in the neighborhood. When they finally tumble into each other on opposite sides of this enormous pumpkin, they strike a deal and everybody is happy. This is a delightful story about pumpkins, Halloween, sharing, and cooperation.

The outline below is a suggested plan for using the various activities that are presented in this unit. You should adapt these ideas to fit your own classroom situation.

Sample Plan

Day 1

- Talk about what it means to share and cooperate. Do Sharing Is Fun activity. (page 21)
- Read and discuss *The Biggest Pumpkin Ever.*
- Draw and write about the biggest pumpkin you can imagine.
- Play Clayton and I Are Friends. (page 44)
- Introduce Sharing Songs. (page 19)

Day 2

- Reread and review *The Biggest Pumpkin Ever.*
- Make a map to show how the mice got the pumpkin to town. (page 20)
- Follow oral directions with listening lesson on pages 22-23.
- Make a Paper Bag Puppet. (page 27) Practice Mouse Math Measurement. (page 24)
- Begin Pumpkin Seed Growth Experiment. (page 26)
- Sing "Sharing in Our Class." (page 67)

Day 3

- Dress up the Paper Mouse Characters. (page 28)
- Continue the Pumpkin Seed Growth Experiment.
- Play Halloween Math Facts Game. (pages 48-50)
- Sing "Sharing with My Neighbor." (page 67)

Day 4

- Find word parts in Halloween Syllables. (page 44)
- Continue Pumpkin Seed Growth Experiment.
- Steam or bake pumpkin seeds. (page 71)
- Continue practicing "Sharing with My Neighbor."

Day 5

- Mold and display clay mice. (page 19)
- Make a Food Collage. (page 25)
- Discuss Pumpkin Seed Growth Experiments.
- Make Halloween Mouse Cookies. (page 69)
- Sing Sharing Songs.

Overview of Activities

Setting the Stage

1. Discuss cooperation and what it means. Let the children tell about ways of cooperating with each other, or about sharing something that was special to them. Make and post a chart of ways we can cooperate in school and at home.

2. Teach the sharing songs on page 67 to the class. Sing "Sharing with My Neighbor" and "Sharing in Our Class." Write the words on butcher or chart paper and post it in the classroom. Add verses about how or when we help each other. Record the songs when children have learned them. Create a listening center in which to play these and other Halloween songs.

3. Let the children make pictures of things they have shared and paste these on a chart or post the chart on a bulletin board and place the pictures around it. Children can write a few sentences about the sharing experience.

4. Have each child complete the Sharing Is Fun activity on page 21. Discuss student responses.

5. Have students draw a picture of the biggest pumpkin they can imagine and write one or more sentences in their journals about it. Tell what you would do with the pumpkin.

Enjoying the Book

1. Read *The Biggest Pumpkin Ever* to the class. Discuss the cooperation between Desmond and Clayton. Ask children to tell about the biggest pumpkin they have ever seen.

2. Let each child find a partner and make one big pumpkin together out of butcher paper or construction paper. Discuss how they can share in decorating it as a jack-o-lantern. Let them make the decisions together and decorate it.

3. Have the children tell you what a pumpkin seed needs to grow. Write the list on a chart and post it in an accessible reading area for children. Start the pumpkin seed experiment on page 26.

4. Discuss the other vegetables from *The Biggest Pumpkin Ever* that were growing in the garden. Write these down on the chalkboard. Have children bring various vegetables to school and have a tasting party. Have the children bring their vegetables in a paper bag. Let each child give one clue about his/her vegetable and the class can guess the name of the vegetable.

5. Have students make Paper Bag puppets as on page 27. Use the puppets to reenact *The Biggest Pumpkin Ever* (or a student created play using a mouse theme).

6. Mold mice from play clay or modeling clay. Use them in diorama settings of *The Biggest Pumpkin Ever.*

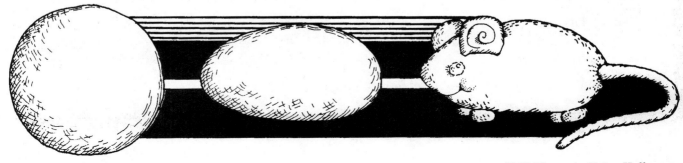

Overview of Activities *(cont.)*

Enjoying the Book *(cont.)*

7. Ask students if they believe mice communicate with each other. Write cartoon captions of what mice might say using suggestions on page 42. Recopy these captions onto heavy paper and let the children dramatize a play using the captions and the Paper Bag puppets on page 27.

8. Use the word list on page 44 to practice syllabication. Students may clap the number of syllables, raise fingers, or put words into pocket chart sections labeled for one, two, or three syllable words.

9. Cook pumpkin seeds following the directions on page 71. Discuss taste, texture, and smell of cooked seeds versus uncooked seeds.

10. Prepare and play the Halloween Math Facts Game as suggested on pages 48-50. Set up a few games at a learning center, or make several sets and have the entire class play in pairs.

11. Learn about the correct usage of the nouns in the subject of a sentence. First, ask each child to name a friend. Put these names on a chart. Next, have students give a sentence about something they enjoy doing together. For example, "Bill and I like to ride our bikes together." Copy it on the chart. Provide additional practice with the "Clayton and I Are Friends" activity on page 44.

12. Do Mouse Math Measurement on page 24. Using metric or standard measurement, have children find the length of the mouse and compare it to other objects in the room. Discuss the results.

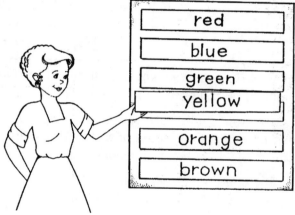

13. Present the listening lesson on pages 22-23. Have students practice following the oral directions given. Tailor the directions to meet student needs.

Extending the Book

1. Color, cut out, and dress up the paper mouse characters on page 28. Use these characters to retell the story. Or, make up and act out a new story about mice using these characters.

2. Write the main events of *The Biggest Pumpkin Ever* on chart paper or make individual books for the children to take home.

3. Using a large piece of butcher paper, design a map showing how the mice got the pumpkin to town. Draw roads and indicate the direction in which they are going. Show houses in the town and the location of the garden.

4. Make a food collage following directions on page 25.

5. Learn about mice. Gather nonfiction books for use in the classroom. Have the class share what they learn.

Name _____

Sharing Is Fun

Think of all the things that you like to share.
Write some of them down in List 1.
Think of all the family and friends you like to share these items with.
Write some of them down in List 2.

List 1

I like to share my:

List 2

I like to share my things with:

Listening Skills

Materials: one jack-o-lantern paper for each student (page 23); pencil; crayons (red, orange, yellow, brown, blue, green)

Directions: The teacher reads the directions one time only. Students are asked to follow the directions.

1. Find the jack-o-lantern with triangle eyes. Color the triangle eyes red.

2. Which jack-o-lantern has a sad face? Color his mouth orange.

3. Find the angry jack-o-lantern. Color his nose brown.

4. Which jack-o-lantern has the longest stem? Color the stem green.

5. Color the mouth of the surprised jack-o-lantern blue.

6. Color the smallest jack-o-lantern orange.

7. Find the happiest jack-o-lantern and color him orange and yellow.

8. Which jack-o-lantern has big eyebrows? Color him three different colors.

Variations: Instead of saying the color words, spell them. Or, hold up cards with the color words written on them and let the children read the words. Or, write the color words on the chalkboard and point to the color word as you read the directions.

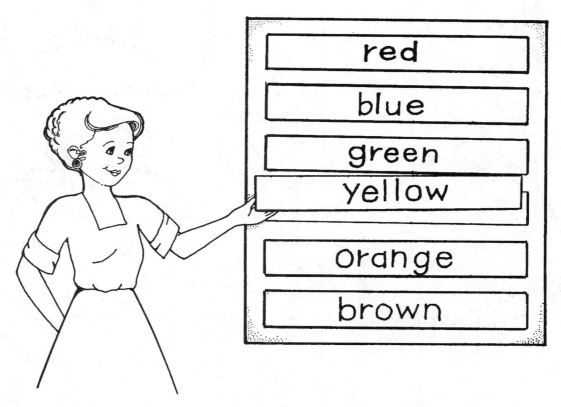

Add compass directions and have the children follow them as you read, i.e., "Color the pumpkin in the northeast corner yellow." Or, use right and left as you describe which jack-o-lantern you want the children to color, i.e., "Color the eyes of the jack-o-lantern in the lower left hand corner blue."

Name _____

Listening Skills *(cont.)*

Directions: Your teacher will tell you exactly what to do on this page. Listen carefully and follow the directions given.

Name _____

Mouse Math Measurement

Measure Maurice the mouse on this page and write down how long he is from the tip of his nose to the end of his tail.

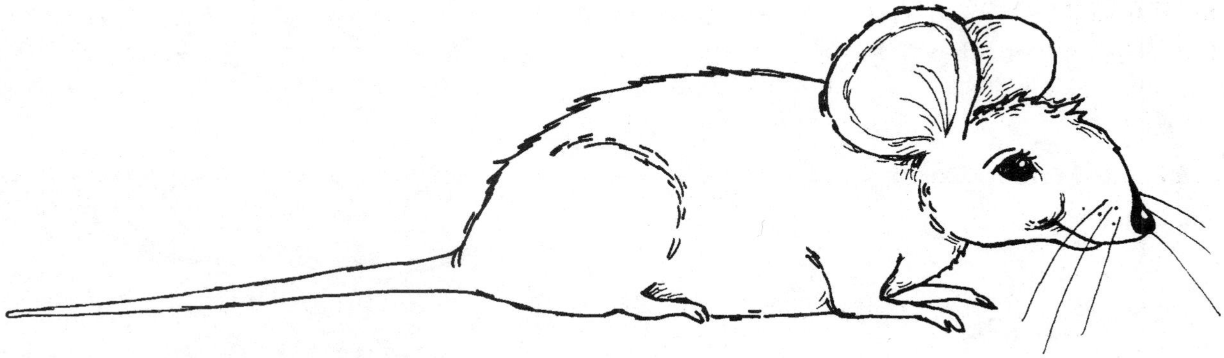

Maurice is about _____ **long.**

What can you find in your classroom that is about the same length as Maurice? Name two objects and write their lengths on the lines below.

Object	Length
_____	_____
_____	_____

Find two classroom objects that are longer than Maurice. Write their names and lengths on the lines below.

Object	Length
_____	_____
_____	_____

Find two objects in the classroom that are shorter than Maurice. Name the objects and write their lengths on the lines below.

Object	Length
_____	_____
_____	_____

Food Collage

Materials: filmstrip projector, overhead projector or lamp; 18" x 24" (45 cm x 60 cm) pieces of black construction paper and white construction paper (one of each per student); chalk or white art pencil; magazines; scissors; glue

Directions: Place a piece of black paper on a wall or chalkboard. Have a child stand in front of the paper (for silhouette) and shine a light source toward the paper. With chalk or white pencil, trace a silhouette of the child's head. Have the student cut out the silhouette and glue it on white paper. Follow the same procedure for each child. Direct students to find and cut out magazine pictures of things they like to eat. Glue them on the silhouette.

Variations: Draw a mouse, cat, bat, horse, etc., on paper and find pictures of things these animals like to eat. Glue the food on the proper animal. Introduce the words *carnivorous, herbivorous,* and *omnivorous.* Write these words on chart paper strips or signs and place them on a bulletin board. Discuss what these words mean and have the children label the animals. Place each animal under the correct heading on the bulletin board.

Pumpkin Seed Growth Experiment

What does a pumpkin seed need to grow? This experiment demonstrates what a plant needs to grow.

Materials: potting soil; 3 large, transparent sealable bags; measuring cup; water; pumpkin seeds; newspaper; permanent marker

Preparation: Label the sealable bags with a permanent marker: 1) DRY SOIL 2) MOIST SOIL 3) WET SOIL

Directions:

- Put one cup of the potting soil on newspaper. Let it sit out in sunlight or on a heater using caution until it is completely dry. (It may take 2-4 days to completely dry out the soil.) Put the dry soil in the plastic bag labeled DRY SOIL. Plant 3-4 seeds in the dry soil and close the bag tightly.

- Place another cup of potting soil in a second bag labeled MOIST SOIL. Plant 3-4 seeds in this bag and close the bag tightly.

- Place another cup of potting soil from the potting soil bag in the third bag labeled WET SOIL. Pour ¼. cup of water in the bag and mix it in with the soil. Plant 3-4 seeds in this bag and seal the bag tightly.

- Place all three bags near a window, but not in direct sunlight. Make a chart and let the children guess which pumpkin will grow the fastest. Discuss what seeds need to grow.

- Do not water the plants for 4 days. Check their growth by carefully opening the bags and peeking in. If nothing has happened in any of the bags, wait 2-3 more days and check again.

- Discuss what happened to each set of seeds and why. (The seeds in the dry soil will not have grown. The wet soil should have produced the most growth.) Explain that seeds need moisture, carbon dioxide, and proper temperature in order to survive and prosper.

Variations: Try this experiment with a fourth "wet soil" bag, but place this bag in a low light or dark area. You could use any type of fast growing seed (zucchini, watermelon, sunflower, lettuce, radish, etc.)

Paper Bag Puppet

Materials: brown paper lunch sack (one per student); scissors; glue; markers or crayons; copies of pattern below

Directions: Reproduce the pattern on this page. Have students color and cut out the patterns. Glue the top of the head on the folded sack's bottom. Glue the mouth part underneath the bottom flap (as shown) so that when a child's hand opens the bottom flap, the mouth is seen.

Paper Mouse Characters

See page 20 for directions and uses.

Arthur's Halloween
by Marc Brown

Summary

Halloween is a bit too scary for Arthur. The decorations in his own house frighten him so much that he can't get to sleep. He doesn't recognize anyone at school in their costumes and everyone enjoys feeling eyeballs (peeled grapes) and brains (cold spaghetti) except Arthur. But worst of all, Arthur has to take D.W., his little sister, trick-or-treating with him. She has no fear and blunders into the scariest house in the neighborhood. At this point, Arthur takes control and ends up enjoying his Halloween adventure very much.

The outline below is a suggested plan for using the various activities that are presented in this unit. You should adapt these ideas to fit your own classroom situation.

Sample Plan

Day 1

- Discuss fear and tell a group story.(page 30)
- Talk about the history of Halloween. (pages 5-6)
- Assemble Small History Book and color pages 1-2. (page 30)
- Introduce and read *Arthur's Halloween.* (page 30)
- Choose a writing idea from the Journal Writing Topics. (page 41)
- Create a classroom haunted house. (page 36)
- Learn the song "Witches, Black Cats, Scary Goblins." (page 68)

Day 2

- Review *Arthur's Halloween* and sequence story events. (page 31)
- Review the history of Halloween and illustrate Small History Book pages 3-4.
- Discuss and draw Arthur's costume.
- Do Bat Math. (page 53)
- Play Halloween Wordo. (page 34)
- Review song from Day 1.

Day 3

- Review Halloween history and illustrate Small History Book pages 5-6.
- Play Alphabetical Halloween. (page 43)
- Make Tissue Paper Goblins. (page 66)

Day 3 *(cont.)*

- Write a greeting card to the old woman in the book. (page 42)
- Play Trick-or-Treat Math. (pages 51-52)
- Do Scary Ticking Noise and Pumpkin Sounds experiments. (page 58)
- Make Witch's Masks in Profile. (page 65)
- Teach "Zip-A-Dee-Do-Dah Halloween" song. (page 68)
- Bake a pumpkin cake. (page 70)

Day 4

- Reread Small History Book and illustrate pages 7-8.
- Create new rhymes from old. (page 39)
- Do Halloween Money experiment. (page 58)
- Make Watercolor Witch's Hat. (page 65)
- Sing and record Halloween songs.

Day 5

- Choose from Journal Writing Ideas on page 41.
- Learn Halloween Adjectives. (page 43)
- Go Trick-or-Treating around Arthur's neighborhood. (pages 59-60)
- Make Goblin Doughouts. (page 69)
- Choose from one of the Culminating Activities on pages 72-73.

Overview of Activities

Setting the Stage

1. Gather Halloween masks and display them in the art center. Also put any symbols of Halloween (black cats, pumpkins, bats, etc.) in this center.

2. Post a map of the British Isles and France. Discuss the history of Halloween using the information on pages 5-6.

3. Assemble and discuss the small history books (pages 32-33) with students. Run copies of pages 32 and 33 back to back. Cut around the outer box in order to trim off the excess edge of the paper. Cut it in half along the dashed line. Place the top half of the page (8,1) over the bottom half (6,3). Fold in half along the book spine, make a cover, and staple.

4. Tell a scary group story. The teacher begins the tale and then points to another student to continue. He/She in turn adds to the story and appoints another child to continue when he/she stops. Continue until one child decides to end the story. You might want to turn out the lights while telling the story.

5. Show the cover of *Arthur's Halloween*. Ask the children to predict what they think this is about. What costume is Arthur wearing? Where do you think he is walking? Does he look happy?

Enjoying the Book

1. Read part of *Arthur's Halloween*. Stop reading just as Arthur goes inside the spooky old house. Ask the children to predict what they think he will find inside. Share predictions with others.

2. Ask students to illustrate and write in their journals what they think Arthur will find inside the house. When completed, have students share their journal writing ideas. Finish reading the book. Discuss Arthur's fears and misconceptions about the "witch."

3. Discuss what type of animal Arthur is (an aardvark). What might this animal do in real life? Have children find out about aardvarks, their habits, where they live, etc.

4. Play Halloween Trick-or-Treater with a partner. One child is a parent and the other child is the trick-or-treater in costume. The trick-or-treater gets down on his knees and holds the hand of the "parent" as they walk along. The child on his/her knees describes how everything looks from a lower height. Exchange places and continue the game.

5. Practice estimation with the Trick-or-Treat Math activity on page 51. Duplicate and cut out the pennies on page 52, or use real pennies. Follow page directions and compare results.

6. Arthur is going trick-or-treating. Discuss safety rules for trick-or-treating and post them in the school. Make copies of pages 59-60. Practice map directions with the class. Let children help Arthur and D.W. find the haunted house as they go trick-or-treating on Halloween.

Overview of Activities *(cont.)*

Extending the Book

1. Sequence the story. Reread the book and list the four main events in random order (A-Arthur goes inside the spooky house; B-Arthur's family gets ready for Halloween; C-Arthur leads his friends through the cemetery; D-Arthur does not enjoy Halloween at school). Have the children divide a paper in fourths and number 1 to 4 in the squares. Beside number one write the letter of the sentence that happened first in the story. Continue until finished. Have children illustrate their answers and check their work.

2. Write Halloween poems. Use the generic frame on page 37 and the poem on page 38 as models. Frame completed poems inside big pumpkins, bats, cats, etc., and display. Or, place in a class book.

3. Write a group letter to a nursing home in your area and ask what the class could do or make for the residents for Halloween. Students could also write letters to nursing home residents using the Halloween Stationery on page 79.

4. Encourage children to look for basic shapes in pictures. Use the drawing lessons on pages 61-63. Copy these pages for the students. Demonstrate the drawings on the chalkboard or an overhead if necessary. Let them write a sentence or story about the characters when they finish their drawings.

5. Talk about the kinds of sounds associated with Halloween. Experiments with sound can be found on page 58.

6. Help students learn sight words using Halloween Wordo (page 34). This can be played as a class or in small groups at a center.

7. Write innovations using the familiar rhymes on page 39 to create new poems. Model an innovation with the class and encourage the students to write their own rhymes using Halloween characters.

8. Review and reinforce the use of adjectives in writing by playing the Halloween Adjectives game on page 43. Make and display charts of descriptive words for Halloween items to be used as word banks for writing activities.

9. Have a Halloween party. Invite some residents from a nursing home. (Make invitations using the Pop-Up Book directions on page 47.) Have visitors watch or help with the vegetable carving and the Halloween drama. See pages 72-73 for suggestions. Serve Goblin Doughnuts, Pumpkin Cake, or any other recipe from pages 69-70 at the party.

Small History Book

See page 30 for directions on assembling the small book pages.

Now we go trick or treating on
Halloween. It is FUN!   8

Halloween started many years ago
in the British Isles and France.   1

Other farmers painted hex signs and
made crosses out of branches to put
on their barns.

6

The Druids believed witches danced
around fires on Halloween night.

3

Small History Book *(cont.)*

See page 30 for directions on assembling the small book pages.

Celtic people and their priests, called Druids, made large bonfires to scare away ghosts.　**2**

Today we don't believe in witches ghosts, or cats that change into people.　**7**

They also believed cats were people changed into cats by evil powers.　**4**

Farmers were scared. They carried torches of fire around their fields to protect their families and animals. **5**

Halloween Wordo

This is a game to help children memorize sight words. It is similar to Bingo. The words can be taken from any of the Halloween books in this unit or from other reading books.

Materials: 8" square board made of construction paper, tagboard, or index paper; game markers (beans, paper squares, etc.); laminate or contact paper; permanent marker; wordo game pattern

Preparation: Cut several boards 8" (20 cm) square. Make copies of the pattern below and glue to the boards. Cover with contact paper or laminate. Using a permanent marker, write a word in each block. Vary the word placement on each card and add one or two different words to each card. (These words can be erased with nail polish remover or ditto fluid and the cards can be reused for additional vocabulary words.) Make a list of all words used on the cards for the caller to use when calling out the words.

Directions: Assign one child to call out the words. The other children cover the words that were called with markers. The first person to have a row of markers in any direction (across, down, or diagonally) is the winner.

Dot-to-Dot Math

Directions: Connect the dots from 1 to 50. Then color me black.

Name _____

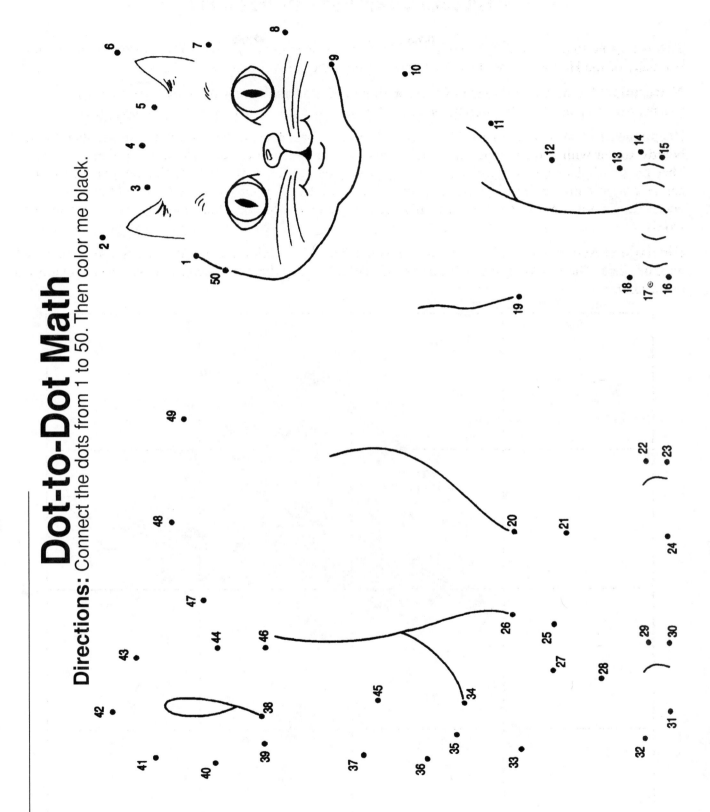

Create A Haunted House

Students will really enjoy making a classroom "Haunted House." Look again at the pictures of the witch's house in *Arthur's Halloween*.

- Discuss and list those things students associate with a haunted house.

- Together make a plan of how the classroom haunted house will look. Design a few rooms using large cardboard boxes opened up as wall partitions, or borrow any available partitions at the school.

- Students in scary costumes can hide in corners or behind partitions to "surprise" any unsuspecting visitors. Play eerie music.

- Decorate the room with hanging goblins and ghosts (see page 66) or other Halloween decorations.

- Place boxes containing mystery items in the rooms. Make sure these items feel slimy, mushy, etc. (Items such as cooked spaghetti, gelatin, shaving cream, and peeled grapes work well.) The boxes should be closed, except for a small opening in one side in which to place the hand and feel the object inside.

- Set up flash lights or dim lighting around the classroom to create a haunted house atmosphere.

Have a frightening good time!

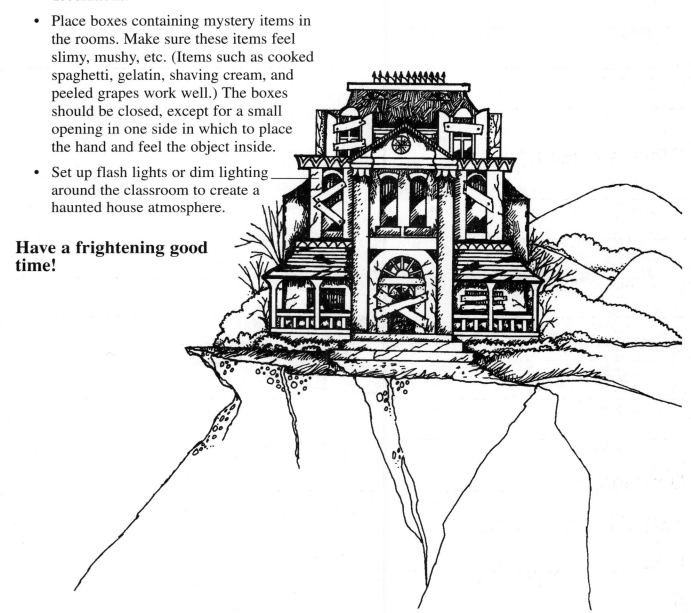

Frame It!

This is a generic frame for a poem. The noun is the subject of the poem. On page 38 this frame is used to create a poem about pumpkins. Encourage students to use the frame to write additional poems of their own.

_____ .
     (noun)

_____ .
     (noun)

_____ .
     (noun)

_____ _____ .
 (adjective)   (noun)

_____ _____ .
 (adjective)   (noun)

_____ _____ _____ _____ .
(adjective) (noun) (adjective) (noun)

_____ _____ _____ _____ .
(adjective) (noun) (adjective) (noun)

These are just a few.

_____ _____ .
(adjective) (noun)

_____ _____ .
(adjective) (noun)

_____ _____ _____ _____ .
(adjective) (noun) (adjective) (noun)

_____ _____ _____ _____ .
(adjective) (noun) (adjective) (noun)

_____ _____ , too .
(adjective) (noun)

_____ _____ .
(adjective) (noun)

_____ _____ .
(adjective) (noun)

Don't forget _____ _____ .
     (adjective) (noun)

Last of all, best of all,

I like _____ _____ .
   (adjective) (noun)

Pumpkin Poetry Frame

This poem uses the generic frame from page 37 with pumpkins as a theme.

Suggested uses: Read and practice the poem with the class. Use the poem for a class choral reading or assign sections to small groups. Illustrate the variety of pumpkins. Label each and display them on a "Pumpkin Poetry" bulletin board. Use the poem as a model for student created poems on Halloween, or any other theme which uses this poetry frame.

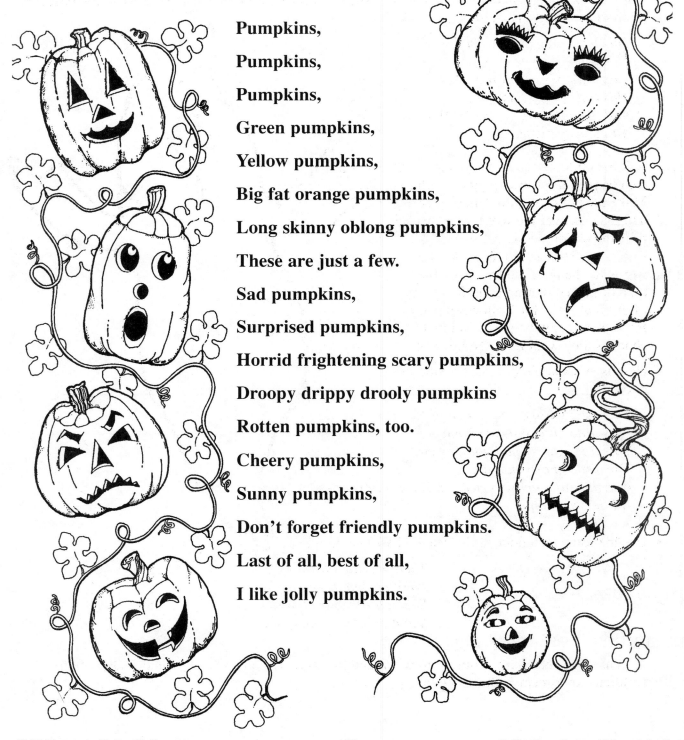

Pumpkins,

Pumpkins,

Pumpkins,

Green pumpkins,

Yellow pumpkins,

Big fat orange pumpkins,

Long skinny oblong pumpkins,

These are just a few.

Sad pumpkins,

Surprised pumpkins,

Horrid frightening scary pumpkins,

Droopy drippy drooly pumpkins

Rotten pumpkins, too.

Cheery pumpkins,

Sunny pumpkins,

Don't forget friendly pumpkins.

Last of all, best of all,

I like jolly pumpkins.

Making New Rhymes From Old

Use the "This Little Piggy" rhyme to help the children see how words can be changed in a rhyme to fit the occasion. Discuss how parents often say this rhyme to babies, pulling their toes or fingers when they get to the last verse. Ask students if they remember hearing this rhyme when they were younger.

Directions:

- Copy the poem on chart paper or sentence strips and place it in a pocket chart. Read the poem and point to the words as you read.

> *This little piggy went to market,*
> *This little piggy stayed home,*
> *This little piggy had roast beef;*
> *This little piggy had none,*
> *And this little piggy cried, "Wee, wee, wee,"*
> *All the way home.*

Ask the children what would happen if we changed the word "piggy" to ghosty. Make a word card with "ghosty" on it and place it over the word piggy each time the children read the word. Encourage students to think of other words to change. Children love this type of poetry writing and often think of original ideas for Halloween poetry. Have them copy the poem and make the changes they want to for Halloween.

Here is an example of a new rhyme using ghosty.

> *This little ghosty went a'haunting,*
> *This little ghosty stayed home,*
> *This little ghosty had goblin stew,*
> *This little ghosty had none,*
> *And this little ghosty cried, "Bo-o-o-o-o-o-o-o-o-!"*
> *All the way home.*

- Use the same technique with "The Old Woman in a Shoe."

> *There was an old woman*
> *Who lived in a shoe.*
> *She had so many children,*
> *She didn't know what to do.*

Try changing the word "woman" to witch and the word "children" to witchlets and let the children experiment with this poem.

Overview of Journal Writing

The term "Journal Writing" refers to the use of blank pages bound together in a book form. Children record their stories, sentences, letters, etc., in the journal on a daily or weekly basis.

Materials: student journals; pencils; crayons; pens; date stamp (optional)

Preparation: Journals can be made very simply out of paper stapled or bound together. The type of paper used can be typing, construction, newsprint, etc. It can be lined or unlined. It can have space for illustrations or not. The cover can be made from the same paper or a heavier paper.

Directions: Throughout this unit the children are asked to write in their journals. It might be copying material from the board or a book, writing words, sentences, or stories. Encourage the children to date their work. This can be done with a date stamp or the children can copy the date themselves. Keeping a record of when each child goes through the writing process is very helpful for the child as well as for your record keeping.

Information: In any class, children will be in various stages of the writing process. In the early stages of writing, children will use scribble writing to tell a story. They can "read" this story to you and you can write it down. Explain to them that they are writing in their own way and you are writing as an adult writes. Later on, the children will often make letters, in a random pattern with no relationship to the sound of the word. The next step is listening to the word and spelling it phonetically. Many children will write the beginning sound of every word when they start spelling. Inventive spelling comes into play here, also. Finally, the child will learn to spell many of the words, form sentences, learn punctuation, and capitalization, and be able to write fluently. If we realize the stages a child goes through in the writing process and let them progress through these stages naturally, children will become writers. And more importantly, they will enjoy writing and use it as another valuable form of communication.

Journal Writing Ideas

The following ideas may be helpful in getting students started with journal entries. These could be posted at a writing center with a suggestion chart on which students can add their own writing ideas.

What scares you? Why?

List the names of all the Halloween costumes you have worn over the years. Which one did you like best? Why did you like it the best?

Describe the costume you are going to wear this year without telling what it is. Pass your journal to a friend or read it aloud and have people guess what you are going to be for Halloween.

Make a picture of your favorite part of a book. Write about it and tell us why you liked it.

Write a recipe for Witch's Brew. What would you put in it? How would you mix it up? Who would drink it?

Describe a bat, a witch, or a goblin in detail.

Where is your favorite place to go trick-or treating? Why do you like it?

You are a witch flying on your broomstick. How do you feel? What do you see? Have you scared anyone?

Describe your magic broomstick. What does it look like?

Tell us everything you know about mice. What do you want to find out about mice?

If you were a witch and could cast a spell, what would your spell be like?

If you were a witch and could grant wishes, what would you wish for? What wishes would you grant your mother, father, sister, and/or brother?

Halloween Writing Projects
Open-ended Sentences

Using pencil, crayons, and lined paper, prepare sentence strips using ideas from the unit books. For example:

> **Corduroy loves**

> **At the party, his friends**

> **If I could go to Corduroy's party, I would**

- Choose a strip containing an open-ended sentence.
- Copy the sentence.
- Add your own ending to the sentence.
- Draw an illustration for the sentence you have finished.

Cartoon Captions

Materials: Caption-shaped balloons made out of newsprint or construction paper; pencils and pens; comic strips for children to look at; copy of the book for which you would like the children to write captions.

Directions: Pose the following question: What would Clayton or the other mice in *The Biggest Pumpkin Ever* say to you if they could talk? Write their comments in the caption balloons.

Greeting Cards

Materials: pencils; scrap paper; crayons, pastels, or markers; colored and white construction paper; scissors; glue

Directions: Send a birthday, get well, thank you, or friendship card to one of the characters in the book. Decorate the card after you have written your message.

Word Games

Alphabetical Halloween

Directions: Present the following activity to the class after reviewing the rules for alphabetizing words. This activity may be done together, in small groups, or individually.

Situation: It's time for a Halloween parade and everyone is lining up in their costumes in alphabetical order. Who comes first in each pair?

ghost or witch	bug or clown
cat or dog	rabbit or owl
skeleton or pumpkin	bear or turtle
vampire or bat	goblin or angel
cowboy or robber	ballerina or monkey
fairy or astronaut	lion or princess
pirate or spider	king or queen

Variations: After the pairs are alphabetized, alphabetize the entire list. If the children come to school in costume, let them alphabetize themselves according to the costumes they are wearing.

Halloween Adjectives

Directions: The object of this game is to have each student think of an adjective that begins with the same letter as his/her Halloween costume. Call on students to introduce themselves in the following way: "I am Gorgeous Ghost;" "I am Bulky Batman;" "I am Skinny Skeleton," etc.

Extension: Let children draw and color pictures of themselves in their Halloween costumes. Add the sentences the children used to introduce themselves. Assemble the student papers into a class book.

Word Games *(cont.)*

These are activities to do when you have an extra minute, want to liven up a reading group, or make that wait in line pass very quickly.

Halloween Syllables

Directions: Pronounce these words and ask the children to tell you the number of syllables in each word by holding up the correct number of fingers. If this is difficult for some children, clap out the syllables as you say the words and let the children clap with you.

Halloween	frightened
witch	spooks
cat	skeleton
black	magic
broom	vampire
goblin	hat
ghost	mask
bat	scary
costume	candy
humbug	haunted
pumpkin	trick
lantern	treat

Clayton and I Are Friends

The object of this game is to let children practice the correct usage of "_____ and I."
Each child thinks of a name of one of his friends. He/she says, "_____and I are friends."
The game continues until all have had a turn.

Variation: Have groups of 5 or 6 students sit in circles. One student chooses a child in the group and says "_____ and I are classmates." The student who was named must repeat the sentence, adding the first child and another child's name. For example, "Adam, Nikki, and I are classmates." Continue until each member of the group has had a turn.

How to Make Big Books

Big Books can be created by students in groups, individually, or as a class. They may contain a pre-determined text, or students may wish to provide both text and illustrations.

Standard Big Book

Bind 12" x 18" (30 cm x 45 cm) pieces of construction paper on the sides or top of paper with rings, holes and yarn, or a binding machine. The cover can be made out of the same paper or any heavier weight paper. Laminate the cover for more durability. This method of construction works with 9" x 12" (23 cm x 30 cm) bound class books as well.

Accordion Books

Use butcher paper, construction paper, or tagboard. Glue together in long strips 9 inches wide or more. They can be as long as you want, but should be folded over every 12 inches. If these books are made on stiff enough paper they will stand up by themselves. The children can arrange them in a circle and sit in the middle and read around the circle. Children really enjoy this!

Shape Books

To make a shape book, cut tagboard in the shape desired for the book's cover (cats, witches, bats, pumpkins, etc). The pages for the book can be cut in the same shape or just cut in squares or rectangles to fit inside the cover. These books can be bound by the same methods used in the standard Big Books.

How to Make Little Books

Children enjoy writing and illustrating their own little books. Follow the directions below and create your own little books.

Materials: construction paper, newsprint, or typing paper; scissors; crayons, markers, pencil

Preparation:

1. Fold the paper in half lengthwise.

2. Fold in half widthwise.

3. Fold in half again widthwise.

4. Unfold the paper. (You should have eight parts now.)

5. Fold in half widthwise.

6. Cut or tear along the center crease from the folded edge to the dot. (See diagram below.)

7. Open the paper.

8. Fold it lengthwise again.

9. Push the end sections together to fold it into a little book.

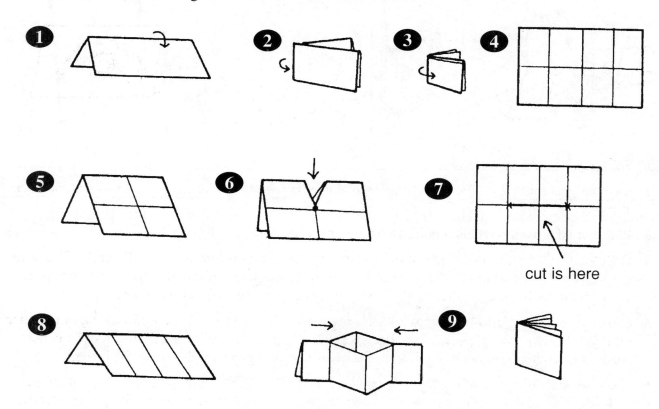

cut is here

Directions: After the children have folded and illustrated the book, let them take turns reading it to you or reading it together in a group. Let them read to a partner. Bring in older students, parent volunteers, or aides to listen to the books. When the children have worked with the book for a day or two, let them take it home to read to their parents.

Pop-Up Books

Use any light color of construction paper to make pop-up pages for the book. You will need a page for each student. For a large class you may wish to put the pages into two books.

Measurements are given for 8½" x 11" (21 cm x 28 cm) paper, but other sizes may be used.

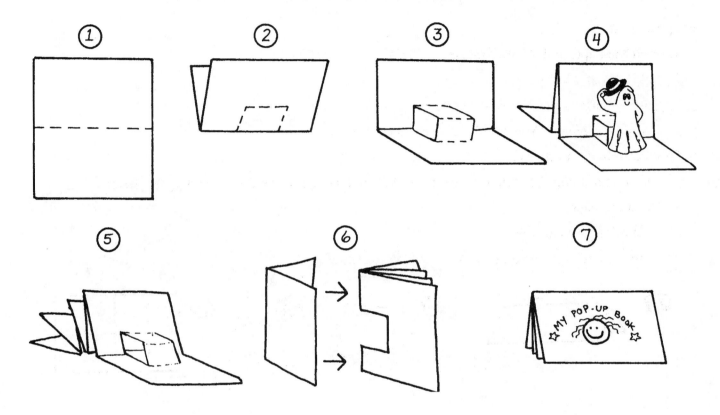

1. Fold paper in half widthwise.

2. Measure and mark 2¾" (7 cm) in from each side along the fold. Cut 2¾" (7 cm) slits at marks as shown.

3. Push cut area inside out and crease to form pop-up section.

4. Have each child draw, color, or cut out something that reminds him/her of Halloween. Glue it to the pop-up portion of the book. Each child may write the name of the picture, a sentence, or a story about his/her picture. This can be written directly on the page or glued on.

5. Glue two pages back-to-back, making sure pop-up section is free. Glue additional pages together until you have a pop-up page for each student. (For invitations, follow steps 1–4. Fold a cover sheet in half widthwise and glue it to the back of the pop-up paper. Decorate the cover.)

6. The cover can be made of tagboard or any heavier paper. It will need to be cut longer than the pages for the book to allow for the extra thickness of the pop-up pages. Glue the cover over the entire book.

7. Add a title and illustrate it.

Halloween Math Facts Game

Materials: Cards and gameboard on pages 49-50; tagboard, file folders, or cardboard; markers (beans, paper, food items, etc.); permanent marker; glue

Preparation: Make one copy of the gameboard and a set of game cards for every two players. Glue the gameboards on tagboard, file folders, or cardboard and cut them out. Laminate. Do the same with the game cards. Write equations on the blank game cards with the marker. When you want to change the game, simply erase the marker with nail polish remover or ditto fluid.

Directions: Put the game cards in a stack. Take the top card from the stack. If you know the answer, say it. Move forward an agreed upon number of spaces. If you don't know the answer, put the card back and move backward one space. The person who reaches the trick-or-treat bag first is the winner.

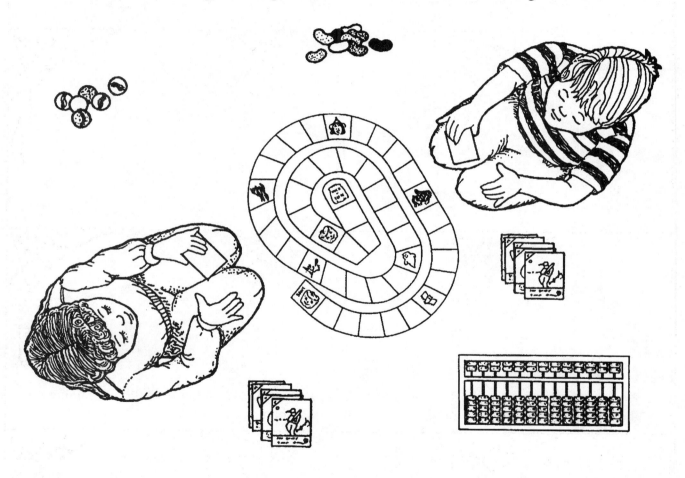

Variations:

- Ask students to make up a simple word problem to fit the equation on the game card.

- Start the game in the center and work to the outside.

- Change the rules. Lose a turn or go back to the beginning if you miss an answer.

Game Cards

See page 48 for directions.

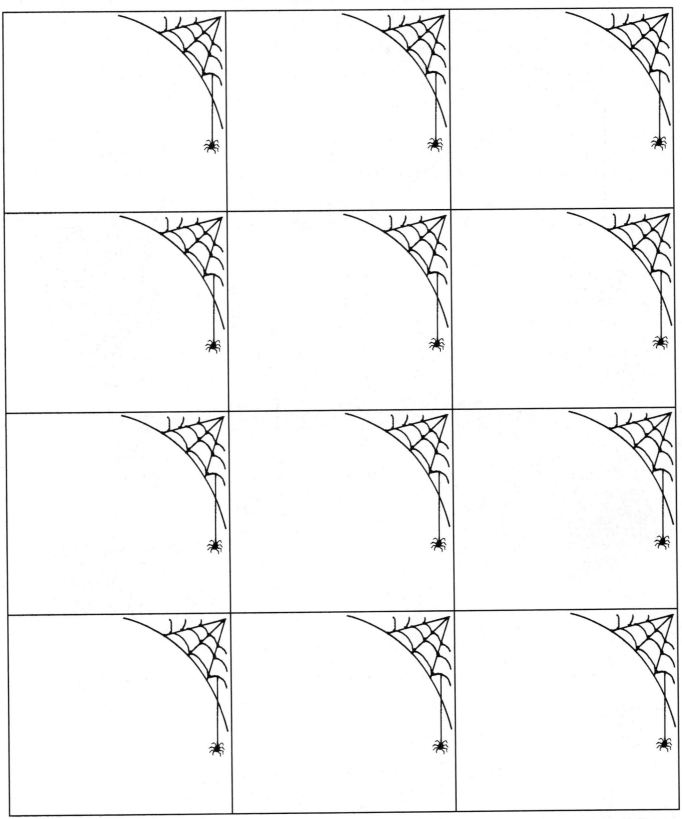

Gameboard

See page 48 for directions.

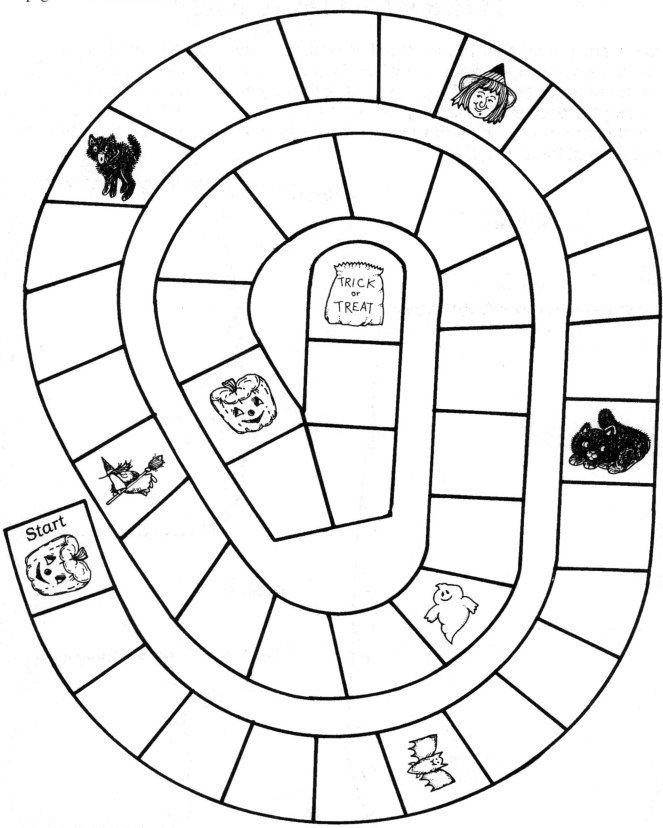

Name _____

Trick-or-Treat Math

How many pennies do you think will fit in trick-or-treat bag A if you put the pennies side by side and fill the whole bag? Make a guess (estimate) first. Cut out the pennies on page 52 (or use real pennies) and fill the bag completely. Check your answer by counting the pennies in bag A. Write the estimate and the actual number of pennies (answer) on the lines next to bag A. Do the same for trick-or treat bags B and C.

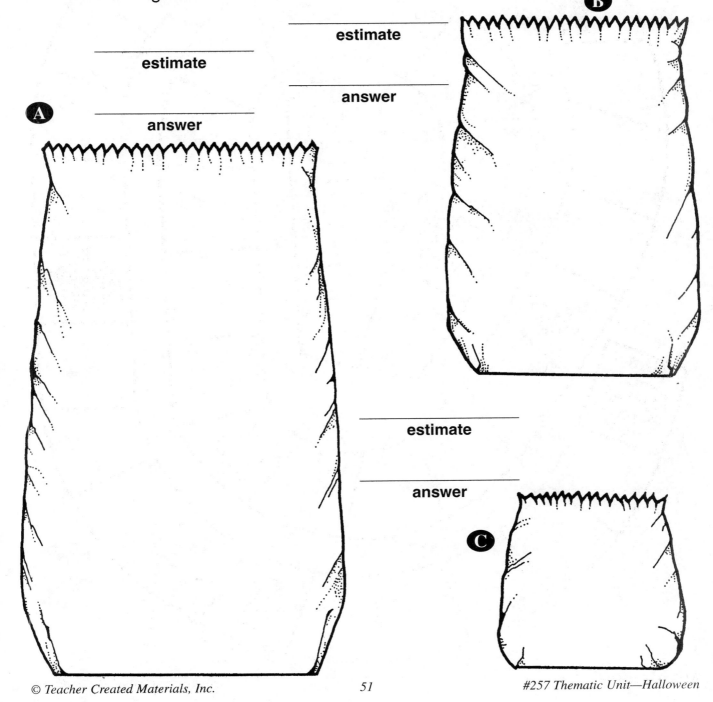

_____
estimate

_____
answer

_____
estimate

_____
answer

_____
estimate

_____
answer

Name _____

Trick-or-Treat Math *(cont.)*

Cut out the pennies on this page and use them to complete the activity on page 51.

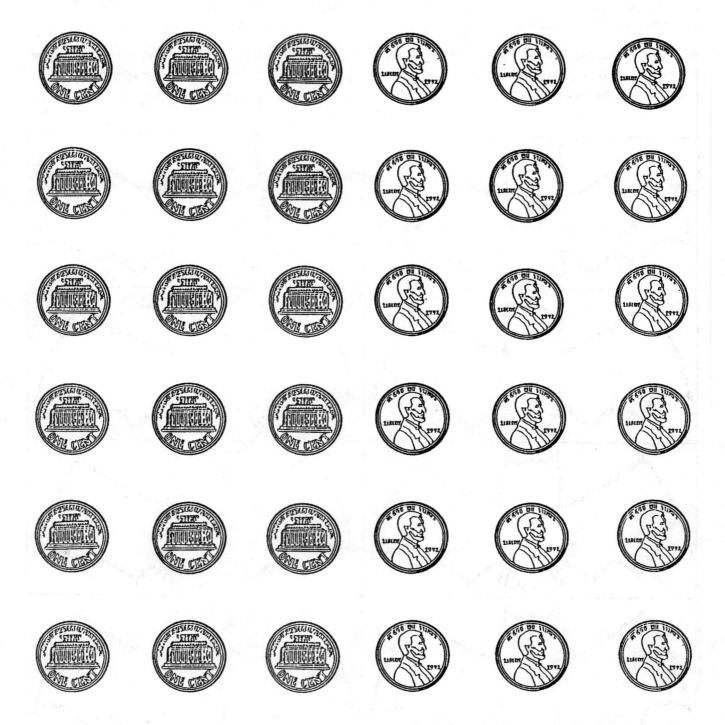

Bat Math

Materials: copies of this page; black construction or butcher paper; scissors; pencils; glue

Teacher Preparation: Write unsolved equations in the bats and make copies of the boxes below. Cut black paper into 3" x 30" (8 cm x 75 cm) strips. Have each child write the answers to the equations on the bats, cut the bat boxes out, and glue them in a horizontal row across the black paper so that answers are shown from least to greatest, or vice versa.

Variations: Change the equations to fit the math facts being taught, to reinforce counting by 2's, S's, or 10's, etc. Run blank copies of the bats and ask students to write their own equations or prepare unsolved equations for classmates.

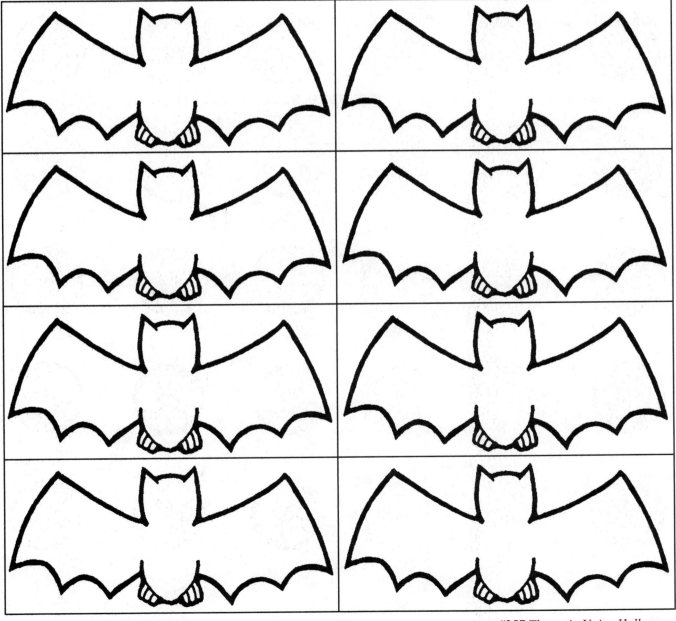

Fall Leaves Me Colder

Corduroy notices the air is growing colder. That is a sign that autumn (or fall) may be near. The air grows colder when the season changes from summer to autumn. This change occurs on the half (or hemisphere) of Earth that is beginning to tilt away from the sun. (At the same time, the season on the other half of Earth is changing from winter to spring because that hemisphere is beginning to tilt toward the sun.) When one hemisphere of Earth is tilted toward the sun, it is summer on that hemisphere. When a hemisphere is tilted away from the sun, it is winter on that hemisphere. When a hemisphere is beginning to tilt toward or away from the sun, it is either spring or autumn on that hemisphere.

Look at the picture below and complete the following statements.

1. The air grows _____ when the season changes from summer to autumn.

2. If it is winter on the Northern Hemisphere, then the Northern Hemisphere is tilted _____ from the sun.

3. During summer on the Southern Hemisphere, the Northern Hemisphere is tilted _____ from the sun.

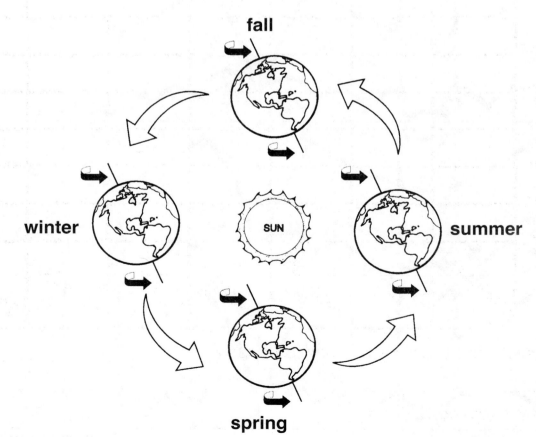

Fall Leaves Me Colder *(cont.)*

Keep a temperature chart during the month of October.

Directions:

1. Find a safe place outside to put your thermometer.
2. Note the temperature at the same time every day for for one week.
3. Color in the bars until you reach the day's temperature.

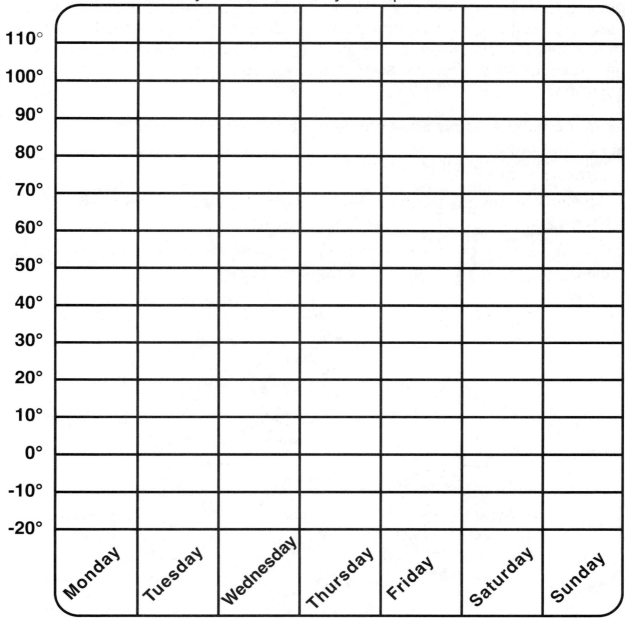

1. Predict what you think is going to happen. _____

_____

2. What happened? _____

Fall Leaves Me Colorful

Color the leaves on this page green, cut them out, and paste them on your tree.
(Teacher: see page 9.)

**1.
Why do leaves change color? Leaves get their green color from a pigment or coloring called chlorophyll that helps them soak up sunlight.**

**2.
Leaves use the energy they get from sunlight, water, and carbon dioxide to make a sugar that the plant uses for food.**

**3.
When leaves produce this sugar, they also give off oxygen.**

Fall Leaves Me Colorful *(cont.)*

Color the leaves on this page orange, red, and yellow. Cut them out and paste them on your tree.

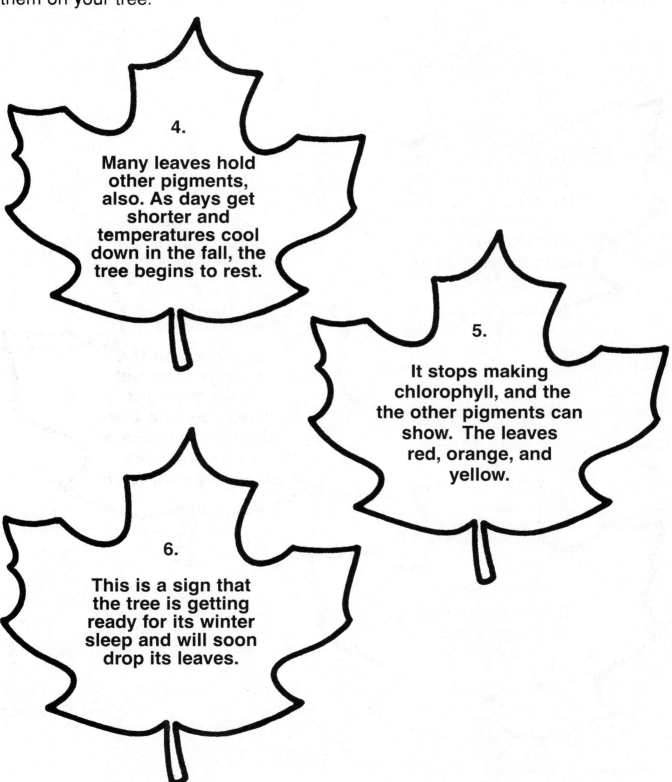

4.

Many leaves hold other pigments, also. As days get shorter and temperatures cool down in the fall, the tree begins to rest.

5.

It stops making chlorophyll, and the the other pigments can show. The leaves red, orange, and yellow.

6.

This is a sign that the tree is getting ready for its winter sleep and will soon drop its leaves.

Halloween Experiments

Scary Ticking Noises

Materials: quiet ticking clock or watch; long piece of wood (such as a wooden cafeteria table, wooden stair railing, or wooden playground equipment).

Directions: Place a watch or clock at one end of the wooden table or railing. Put your ear down tightly on the other end of the table. Place a hand over your other ear. Can you hear the ticking? Is it louder or softer when you put your ear to the wood?

Explanation: Sound waves travel faster and better through hard solids than through liquids or gases. They travel more than 10,000 feet per second in wood as opposed to about 1100 feet per second in air. This is because in solids the molecules are closer together and carry sound vibrations more quickly.

Pumpkin Sounds

Materials: two identical plastic pumpkins, one ticking watch or quiet clock

Directions: Place one pumpkin on your desk upside down and put a watch or clock on top of it. Hold the other pumpkin (with the opening against your ear) just above the watch, but not touching it. Where do you hear the ticking sound? Try placing the watch inside the pumpkin on the desk. Experiment with different positions of the watch and pumpkins.

Explanation: The watch will sound like it is ticking in the pumpkin by the ear because sound bounces off surfaces. This is an echo. Ask the children to watch for cone shaped T.V. antennas. They operate on the same principal.

Halloween Money

Materials: a coin that someone gave you for Halloween, or any coin; a straw; glass of water

Directions: Find a partner. Put the coin on a table. Dip the end of your straw in the water. Put the straw down on the coin and suck up. Lift the coin up while you are sucking. Wipe the coin dry. Let your partner try sucking up the coin without dipping his straw in water. Does the coin come up?

Information: Water sticks to itself and forms a cohesive bond. Water also seals the straw to the coin so when you suck in through the straw you reduce the air pressure inside the straw. Water is also attracted to the straw and the coin by adhesion.

Trick-or-Treating

Directions: Use the compass and steps on this page to help Arthur and D.W. find the "haunted house" in their neighborhood. You can play this game by yourself or with a partner (taking turns following the directions). Use a pencil or marker to trace the path on the map (page 60).

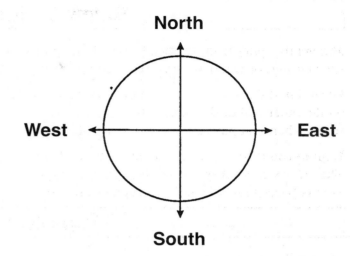

Steps:

1. Find Arthur and D.W. Take them WEST on Bat Avenue.

2. Go NORTH on Goblin Street.

3. Stop at the first house on your right and go treat-or-treating.

4. Continue NORTH on Goblin Street.

5. Go EAST on Witch Avenue and then SOUTH on Black Cat Street.

6. Stop at the corner house with the swimming pool.

7. Go up the path to this house. You have found the haunted house! Go trick or-treating.

8. Now find your way back home through the graveyard. Which direction are you going? Happy Halloween!

- -

Teacher Note:

1. Have students make their own maps from their house to where they want to go trick-or-treating. Include directions. Let a partner find his/her way around using the map.

2. Take the class on a "Direction Walk." Write directions on cards and let the class follow them to a neighborhood house or home of one of your students. Do not tell them ahead of time where you are going. Let them read the directions and make a prediction about where they think the map is taking them. If possible, use compasses on the walk.

Trick-or-Treating *(cont.)*

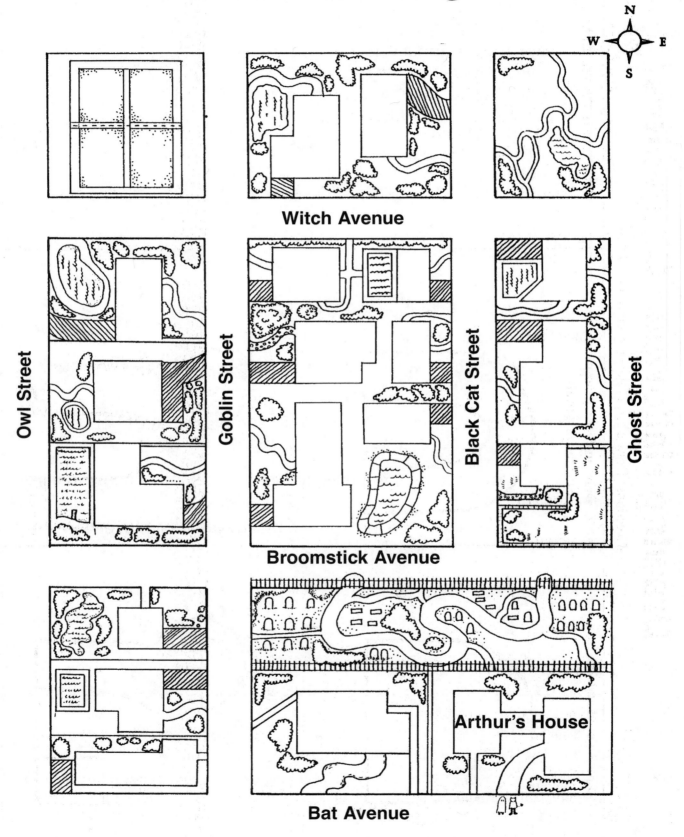

Witch Avenue

Owl Street

Goblin Street

Broomstick Avenue

Black Cat Street

Ghost Street

Arthur's House

Bat Avenue

Drawing Halloween Characters

Directions: Draw a cat. Follow the steps in each box.

Draw your Halloween cat here.

1. Draw half of an oval.

2. Draw another half oval inside the first oval

3. Add eyebrows, eyes, nose, mouth, and ear shapes as shown.

4. Complete your cat with whiskers and hair to make your cat look scary.

Drawing Halloween Characters *(cont)*

Directions: Draw a bat. Follow the steps in each box.

Draw your Halloween bat here.

1. Draw a long oval body.

2. Add a triangle for each wing.

3. Add zig zag lines on the bottom of each wing. Give your bat triangle ears and feet.

4. Add oval eyes, a smile and triangle teeth. Where is your bat going?

62

Drawing Halloween Characters *(cont)*

Directions: Draw a witch. Follow the steps in each box.

Draw your own witch here.

2. Add an oval head. Put a skinny oval on top for a hat brim and add a triangle top.

4. Add hair, a face, and a broom.

1. Draw an oval for the body.

3. Draw a set of connecting ovals for arms, legs, hands, and feet.

Halloween Weaving

Materials: black 12" x 18" (cm x 45 cm) construction paper; strips of various widths of orange construction paper cut into 12" lengths; scissors; glue; pencil

Directions: Have students follow the steps below to create their own weaving pattern.

1 Fold the black paper in half widthwise.	**2** Draw a parallel pencil line 1" (2.54 cm) from the open edges.
3 Cut curved, straight, or zig-zag lines from the fold up to the 1" line. Open the paper.	**4** Weave strips of orange paper across the width of the black paper. Experiment leaving spaces, going under one, over two, etc.

When the design is complete, have students glue the ends of the strips down and trim off the extra.

Variations: Try weaving with any color paper, or use magazines, newspaper, or wallpaper cut in strips. Weave ribbon, yarn, or straw into the picture.

Bewitching Art

Witch's Mask in Profile

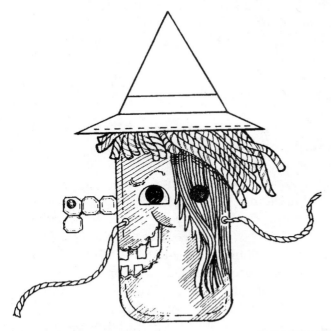

Materials: large paper egg carton (18 egg size); black construction paper; yarn; stapler; scissors; tempera paint, color of choice

Directions: Cut the top off a large egg carton. Paint this part green, brown, or any color you want the witch to be. Cut 4 egg cups off and paint them the same color. Glue the cups in an "L" shape for a nose and staple to the carton top. Cut eyeholes and paint an eyebrow above one eye hole. Paint hair around the other eye hole. Attach yarn over the top for more hair. Paint a smile or cackle mouth and crooked teeth. Staple a black pointed hat to the top. Paint a black wart on the nose. Attach yarn to the edges as shown to wear the mask.

Watercolor Witch's Hat

Materials: white 9" (23 cm) square construction paper; tagboard; triangle shapes for tracing; black crayons; watercolor paints and brush; water; black or orange paper for mounting; pencil

Directions: Ask children to think about an interesting design they can make using the shape of a witch's hat (triangle). This shape can overlap, point in any direction, or be used in any way on the paper. Trace the shapes on your white paper with a pencil and then outline them with a black crayon. Paint each shape with orange or black watercolor paints. Mount your design on black or orange paper.

Variations: Have copies of all the basic shapes and let the children choose one shape only to use on their design. Experiment with various colors and combinations of shapes.

Haunting Halloween Decorations

3-D Ghost

Materials: 30" (70 cm) squares of cheese cloth (two per student); fabric stiffener (available at craft or fabric stores); white glue; scissors; margarine cups or other disposable bowls; plastic wrap (about 2 feet per student); 8 oz. (236 mL) plastic or foam cups; paper tape; black felt; aluminum foil; plastic bags to cover work area.

Directions: Roll a piece of aluminum foil into a 2" (5 cm) ball shape. Tape it to the bottom of a paper or foam cup (this becomes the ghost figure). Place the figure upside down on the plastic bag and cover it with plastic wrap. Place one square of cheese cloth over the other for double thickness. Dip the cheese cloth (fold into quarters or eighths first) into a bowl of fabric stiffener and squeeze out excess. Unfold and drape cheese cloth over the plastic wrapped figure. Crimp edges and shape to create desired effect. Let dry overnight. Lift from mold and glue felt eyes and mouth on. Add accessories.

Tissue Paper Goblin

Materials: tissue paper of various colors; liquid starch; paint brush; 9" x 12" (23 cm x 30 cm) white construction paper; newspaper for working area

Directions: Tear tissue paper for parts of the goblin's body. Brush the white construction paper with starch. Lay on the parts of the goblin. Put a coat of starch over each part of the body. Decorate the room with the goblins.

Variations: Use scissors instead of tearing for a less scary look. Use orange tissue paper to make the body of the goblin and put it down first with starch. Dress the goblin with torn tissue paper clothes. This method could be used to make a pumpkin, witch, person in costume, or any animal.

Songs

"Corduroy's Fall Song"

Sing this song to the tune of *"Jingle Bells."*

Cor-du-roy,
Cor-du-roy,

Fall is finally here.
The air is cold,

The clouds appear,
It's changing, little bear!

Leaves will change
Red, orange, brown;
They fall to the ground.

Soon the moon shines big and bright
For fall is finally here.

Variations: Encourage the children to make additional verses about what happens during the fall season.

"Sharing in Our Class"

Sing this song to the tune of *"The Wheels on the Bus."*
The sharing in our class goes 'round and 'round,
'Round and 'round, 'round and 'round. The sharing in
our class goes 'round and 'round,
We all share together.

"Sharing with My Neighbor"

Sing this song to the tune of *"I'm a Little Teapot."*

> *Sharing is a good thing,*
> *Yes, indeed.*
> *I'll share with my neighbor,*
> *I'll share with my friend.*
> *Sharing is a good thing,*
> *Yes, indeed.*
> *I feel good when I share with you.*

Variation: When you sing the last line, replace "you" with a child's name. Point to a child as you sing the song and everyone adds his/her name at the end. Or, hold up a child's name and the children read the name and sing it on the last line.

Songs *(cont.)*

"Witches, Black Cats, Scary Goblins" by Marita Graube

Sing this song to the tune of *"Frere Jacques"*

Witches, black cats,
Scary goblins,
Hal-lo-ween!
Hal-lo-ween!
Let's go Trick-or-Treating!
Let's go Trick-or-Treating!
Oh! What fun!
Oh! What fun!

"Zip A-Dee-Do-Dah Halloween"

Sing this song to the tune of *"Zip-A-Dee-Do-Dah."*

Halloween costumes,
Halloween play,
My! Oh! My! What a frightening day!
Plenty of scary stuff
Coming my way.
Halloween fun on
Halloween day.

Mr. Black Bat on my shoulder,
It's the truth,
It's factual,
Everything isn't satisfactual
(Repeat chorus)

Mrs. Black Cat by my leg,
It's the truth,
It's factual,
Everything isn't satisfactual.
(Repeat chorus)

Variations: Let the children help make up new verses for these songs. Add movement to the lyrics.

Goblin Good Snacks

Halloween Mouse Cookies

Materials: homemade cookies from a favorite recipe; chocolate peppermint wafers; chocolate chips; toothpicks

Directions: Make a batch of plain cookies (such as sugar or butter cookies). As soon as the cookies come from the oven, place a chocolate peppermint wafer in the center of each. Place two chocolate chips next to the mint for the mouse's head and ears. Place one chocolate chip on the bottom of the mint for the tail. With a toothpick, shape the melting chocolate pieces into a head, ears, and tail of your mouse.

Variations: Buy cookies and let the children place the chocolate chips on the cookies and then heat them up. Place cookies in a microwave for 10-15 seconds or until the chocolate melts. Pass out to the children very quickly before the chocolate cools and hardens. Let them shape the chocolate with the toothpicks. Caution them that melted chocolate is hot. Do not touch it with your fingers. Use the toothpicks.

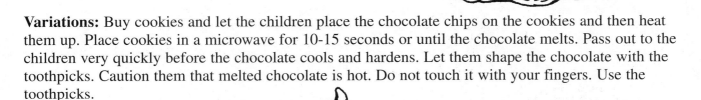

Goblin Doughnuts

Materials: one loaf frozen bread dough; flour; knife; salad oil; cookie sheet; wax paper; frying pan or electric skillet; cinnamon sugar; spatula; paper towels; rolling pin (optional)

Directions: Thaw the bread dough as package directs. This will take 2 to 3 hours. Cut thawed loaf crosswise and lengthwise to make enough so each student will have one piece.

Give each child a sheet of wax paper, some flour, and a piece of dough. Let the children roll, flatten, fold, knot, or cut the dough to make any shape they want. Let the dough rise in a warm place until it is very light and puffy, about 30 minutes.

Put 1½ inches of salad oil in the skillet. Heat to 350 degrees Fahrenheit (180 degrees Celsius). Fry 4 to 5 pieces of dough at a time. Turn the dough as needed until golden on all sides (about 2 minutes). Remove from oil and drain on paper towels. Coat doughnuts in cinnamon sugar. Before the children eat the doughnuts, let them decide what their shape looks like and give it a name. They might want to make a picture of it and write a sentence about it.

Goblin Good Snacks *(cont.)*

Pumpkin Milkshakes

Materials: blender; measuring cup and spoons; paper cups

Ingredients:

2 cups (470 mL) cooked or canned pumpkin	1 tsp. (5 mL) cinnamon
½ cup (118 mL) brown sugar	1 tsp. (5 mL) nutmeg
½ cup (118 mL) granulated sugar	1 tsp. (5 mL) vanilla
3 to 4 cups (700-940 mL) of evaporated milk	

Put all the ingredients in a blender in the order given. Place in layers. Do not stir. At this point, have the children predict what color they think the final product will be. Let the children watch as the blender mixes the colors.

Variations: Before blending, make a chart and have the children sign their names below the color they think the milkshake will be after it is blended.

Pumpkin Cake

Materials: mixing bowl; measuring cup and spoons; oblong cake pan; egg beater or whip; large spoon
Ingredients:

1 pkg. spice cake mix	2 cups (472 mL) canned pumpkin
2 eggs	½ cup (118 mL) milk
1 tsp. (5 mL) baking soda	

Mix all ingredients in bowl. Pour the batter into a greased cake pan. Bake at 350 degrees Fahrenheit (180 degrees Celsius) for 25-30 minutes or until golden brown or toothpick inserted in cake comes out clean. For a special treat, serve with a scoop of ice cream!

Goblin Good Snacks *(cont.)*

Cooking a Pumpkin

Many children have never seen a pumpkin being cooked. Letting them participate in this project helps them realize how it is prepared.

Materials: pumpkin; large spoons; sharp knife; newspapers; bowls; pan

Directions: Cut the top off a pumpkin to make a lid. Clean out the seeds and strings. Set the pumpkin in a pan of water in the oven at 350 degrees Fahrenheit (180 degrees Celsius) for about one hour, or until sides of pumpkin are soft when pierced with a fork.
Give the children a spoonful of pumpkin to smell, taste, and touch. What would they do to prepare the cooked pumpkin meat for a pie? Discuss this and let the children write about it.

Steamed and Baked Pumpkin Seeds

Materials: pumpkin seeds; steamer; cookie sheet; oil; salt

Steaming softens the outer part of the seed and makes it less tough. Place the seeds in a steamer and cook them 20-30 minutes over water. Cover the pot and add more water if needed. Steaming can be eliminated, if you haven't time.

Place the seeds on a towel and pat them dry. Spread them out on a cookie sheet. Add a little oil and stir the seeds. Sprinkle with salt and bake at 300 degrees Fahrenheit (180 degrees Celsius) for about 30 minutes or until golden brown and crispy.

Halloween Vegetable Carving

Instead of, or in addition to, carving pumpkins, try other types of squash, gourds, apples, turnips, potatoes (white or sweet), or thick carrots.

Materials: vegetables for carving; knives; newspaper; spoons; a row of small Christmas tree lights (optional)

Directions: Ask children to bring in a vegetable. Let them describe it to the class. Or, they could place it in a paper bag. Give one clue about it and let children take turns guessing the name of the vegetable. Let children work with partners or have children work individually on the carving. After all vegetables are carved, place them in a row and add decorative lighting with tiny Christmas tree lights. Distribute Halloween Costume Awards (page 76) for the funniest, most creative, wisest, meanest looking, oddest, etc., vegetable. Every carving should get an award of some type. The children can help decide what to write on the award certificate or the teacher can do this independently.

Variations: Have a vegetable parade and let the children parade around the school with their carved vegetables. Or, arrange a time for other classes to come and visit your display. Write stories about the vegetables. Make up a song or poem about them. Make pictures of the vegetables and place these on the bulletin board or bind them into a book. These activities will need to be done within a couple of days, because the vegetables start to mold and it's best to send them home before that happens.

Cooperative Halloween Mini-Plays

Ask the children to bring their Halloween costumes to school. Before they put on their costumes, have each child tell what he/she is going to be for Halloween and what he/she thinks that character would act like if it were real.

Have children put on costumes and let the children find a partner they would like to work with. Have them close their eyes and visualize what they think these characters could do together. Where are they going? What are they doing? What noises or sounds do they make?

Have groups of students prepare mini-plays using their costume and props. Allow enough time for groups to work out their scenes.

Let the children problem solve what props they need and how they can make or improvise these items. Give them time to make props and practice using them in their scenes.

Discuss projecting your voice so all can hear. Practice speaking into a pretend microphone. Record the plays and let students listen to the sound. Was it loud enough? Could your audience hear you? Did you speak clearly and pronounce every word?

Encourage children to think about the following questions while performing: What motions will my character make? How will I use my hands, arms, legs, feet, head, shoulders?

Videotape the performances. Take pictures and post in the classroom. Let children write stories about the pictures and stories. Bring the class back together and let the groups perform for an audience. Choose new partners and repeat. Invite other classes, parents, school staff, and administrators to see your performances.

Variations: Mix up costumes. Place the mask from one costume onto another child's costume. Trade props or parts of costumes. Let the group make up stories about these new characters. Can they name them? What sounds would this new creature make? Let all the children act out how this character would walk, talk, and move.

Letters to Parents

Teacher Directions:

Send the top letter with the first Little Book you send home. When Big Books are ready to be sent home, secure them in large plastic bags. Attach the note at the bottom of this page with clear contact paper to the bags that contain the Big Books.

Dear Parents,

Today your child is bringing home a Little Book. This Little Book is a miniature of the books, poems, or charts that we use in our classroom. The Little Book is for you to enjoy with your child. Let your child "read" the book to you. Don't worry if your child doesn't have all the right words or if he or she is memorizing the text. This is how reading starts. Celebrate what your child can do and the interest shown in wanting to learn to read.

Thank you for taking the time to share the Little Book. Your involvement is critical to your child's success.

Sincerely,

_____
Teacher's signature

Dear Parents,

I am bringing this Big Book home to read to you. Please take time to listen to me read it and help me to remember to return it to school tomorrow.

Thank you.

74